A Bibliography
of the Writings of
James Branch Cabell

James Branch Cabell

A Bibliography
of the Writings of
James Branch Cabell

By
Guy Holt

PHILADELPHIA

THE CENTAUR BOOK SHOP

1924

HASKELL HOUSE PUBLISHERS Ltd.

Publishers of Scarce Scholarly Books

NEW YORK, N. Y. 10012

1972

HASKELL HOUSE PUBLISHERS Ltd.

Publishers of Scarce Scholarly Books

280 LAFAYETTE STREET

NEW YORK, N. Y. 10012

Library of Congress Cataloging in Publication Data

Holt, Guy, 1892-1934.
    A bibliography of the writings of James Branch Cabell.

    Original ed. issued as no. 3 of The Centaur biblio-
graphies of modern American authors.
    1. Cabell, James Branch, 1879-1958--Bibliography.
I. Series: The Centaur bibliographies.
Z8139.7.H75 1972   016.813'5'2   72-757
ISBN 0-8383-1424-4

ABOUT THESE BOOKS

By James Branch Cabell

PON a number of counts, I prefer here to say nothing about these books. Apart, entirely, from much inner monitory whispering as to the aureate qualities of silence, I have found the minuteness and split hairs — the superfine orthology and the paraded cantlets and flitters — of the bibliographic art, when in full exercise, to beget in its beholders speechlessness. . . Nobody will I hope, misunderstand my meaning. With all appropriate awe and admiration I have considered intricate mathematical research as to the number of existent "states" of *The Eagle's Shadow*, and concerning how many copies of *From the Hidden Way* display upon the backbone an underlined C. I have applauded the nicety with which one can distinguish to a quarter-inch between the second and first printing of *Jurgen*. I have been suitably perturbed over the prestige imparted by a blue binding to *The Soul of Melicent* as compared with the sable investure of relative parvenus. And I have, rather naturally, rejoiced that this meticulous method of cataloguing in legible print all my least deeds and misdeeds as a writer does not, even more embarrassingly, invade the field of my actions as a human being. . . It is, in fine, my appreciation, rather than any crass derisory estimate, of such painstaking

in our superficial world, that troubles me.   It is as inde-
fatigation's beholder that I am left, really, speechless.

And, for another matter, I would prefer here to say
nothing about these books because thus only might I avoid
confessing that, were the choice afforded me, no one of
these first editions hereinafter anatomized would to-day
exist.   That I perceive to be, as a gambit, maladroit.   I,
none the less (not all unbiased), cannot but view these
first editions with distaste, even shudderingly, as abortions
begotten by the depravity of the compositor upon the in-
competence of the author.   The emotions roused in me
by a first edition of *Beyond Life* or of the revised *Cords
of Vanity* are, in fact, not the sort of thing that can be
printed.

These two are in the infirmary of my collected works
the worst cases.   But in viewing any one of these first
editions I am signally condemned to consider the mis-
prints, and the more dire untypographic blunders that are
due to auctorial noddings, in rather the frame of mind in
which one fidgets through the familiar nightmare of at-
tending a public gathering, cynosurally, in one's sleeping
attire.   And nowhere could I more pleasurably warm, in
the old phrase, the very cockles of my heart than beside a
bonfire whose fuel was every existing copy of these first
editions.   .   .

Yet that is worded over-rashly.   For I would perforce
protest against destruction of *From the Hidden Way*,
which I admit to be, for reasons utterly unliterary, my
favorite among my books; and toward which my senti-
ments are so disastrously unique that nobody anywhere
has ever suggested a second printing.   But the others I

would incinerate — elatedly and in, as people mystically put it, the twinkling of a bed post — now that a revised and an approximately corrected version of each one of them exists, to fall (by however little) a whit less short of the Intended Edition which will not ever, quite, be completed. . .

Yet of the Intended Edition, also, it seems that I might wiselier here say nothing; and thus avoid confessing that, even in a bibliography, to list these books according to the date of publication disquiets me. Commencement with *The Eagle's Shadow*, for example, appears, to me, most clamantly unreasonable in the light of my flaming private conviction that *The Eagle's Shadow* is, in truth, the fifteenth chapter of the longish Biography upon which I am yet engaged. This point I shall not argue, though, not even with appeals to the prevalent assemblage of the Leather Stocking saga or of the *Comédie Humaine* or of the works of Rabelais. It seems too generally agreed that, when I speak of my separate publications as the chapters of one book, my babblings are attributable, at the auditor's choice, to affectation or insanity. I privily retain my notion, then, that with the completing, and the fitting into their niches, of some four more chapters, this Biography may yet reveal the coherence of a not unplanned nor wholly accidental edifice. But I retain my notion tacitly: and I elect to blurt out, in my impulsive unconsidered way, nothing further about it here, lest, here again, I wander into over-rash declarings. . .

In fine, I discover on every side the impossibility of saying anything about the various items of this particular bibliography without asserting rather more than I have leisure to substantiate or second thoughts to endorse. Therefore I skuttle toward shelter in the umbrageous, shielding depths of a jungle of orotundity.

The trouble may well be — here to resort to candor as the likeliest forceps with which to extract the teeth of detection — that I at times regard these books almost quite seriously. And I dare even venture to palliate my attitude. For, these books are, I must however unwillingly admit they are, not merely frivolous æsthetic trivialities, not merely dissolute time-wasting in the wanton fields of what some of us (in Dr. P. E. More's fine phrase) "are pleased to call art." These volumes represent, just as they stand, the increment of such assets in the way of imagination and industry and youth and health as were, two decades since, my sole endowments. Each one of these endowments has been given, utterly, throughout some twenty years, to the making of these books: one all the while, as an Economist, regarding this disposal of one's assets as upon the whole a possibly judicious hazard. These books, just as they stand, thus represent the dividends and accrued interest of their writer's annual investments; and therefore should by level-headed persons, I submit, be regarded with the unfrivolity appropriate not (heaven knows!) to any "artistic" nonsense, but to the outcome of a business transaction. For the Biography is really a matter of finance, in that man-handled word's first meaning. And in a business transaction, failure has its graver aspects, and not even the most imperilled investor goes under bond to be wholly free of seriousness.

So I confess that, here again for reasons utterly unliterary, I regard each one of the increments of my long-

standing investment with a naïve and unhidden seriousness. They are diverse. A number in no way resemble
reading-matter. That perhaps is why — just as I stated
at outset — I prefer, for more reasons than one can have
at only ten finger-tips, here to say nothing about these
books. And I have, I hope, indulged this preference.

Dumbarton Grange
January 1924

PREFACE

I HAVE been asked by The Centaur Book Shop for a note of introduction to this bibliography of the writings of James Branch Cabell, and I find myself at a loss for any word other than in evasion or apology. For today, as it so happens, I have run through some score or more of press cuttings of reviews of two of Cabell's books — his first and his latest — and I find expressed in them almost every conceivable opinion that may be held of a man's work; and, reflecting that these are but a few samples of the criticism which has been devoted to Cabell in the past five years, I hold it the part of wisdom to refrain from any exposition of, or comment upon, the books of which this bibliography is the genealogical record.

So much by way of evasion. For the rest, I have attempted to make of this book a complete and accurate accounting of the published writings of Cabell, with such physical descriptions as will enable the collector to identify first editions of each of his books. Happily, that is a task of no great difficulty; for human imperfection and the perversity of printers (and of publishers) have conspired to differentiate the first issues of each book from its less faulty successors. Thus you will find, here, a seated heroine, there, a definite article mislaid, elsewhere, a letter *c* fallen from its proper level, each contriving to flout uniformity and contributing to a Comedy of Variations, to which Mr. Cabell, by means of endless revisions and emendations, has generously added. I might, indeed, with some show of justice have hereinafter listed separately almost every one of the editions and impressions of Cabell's various books, for in few of them has he failed to make several minor textual changes. That I have not done so will, I trust, make no one quarrel with me. I have included only those reprints which contain major revisions of the original text, and even in the case of the first English edition of *Jurgen*, I have refrained from giving an extended description of the book, contenting myself with a note upon its variations from the American text.

Finally, I must here express my thanks to Mr. Cabell for his assistance without which this record would not yet be completed, and to Mr. Harold Mason and to Mr. David Jester, for their patience in the face of many delays.
December 26, 1923

*   *   *   *   *   *

At this point, several weeks ago, I concluded the prefatory note which seemed, at that time, to express all that I had to say upon the subject of Mr. Cabell's books. Now I am moved to add a postscript to the record, and, quite unapologetically, to deal with sundry omissions of which I have been guilty. For I learn that the true Bibliophile is a very Lazarus, and no crumbs are ungrateful to him; and I must, therefore, make mention of certain opuscula which, through inadvertence or mischance, I have failed to mention hereinafter.

How far my ignorance has gone toward making imperfect this record I cannot say. That it includes every work of which Mr. Cabell or I had any recollection, goes without saying. But, though a man's writings are more voluminous than his works, they exceed by little his publications; and let a scrap of original matter once find its way into print, be it a stray commendation of another's book, an inscription in his own, or even a couplet written for a menu, that trifle becomes a part of the author's contribution to literature and its original repository a legitimate "item" for the collector.

Well, be it known, then, that I am guilty in these respects. I have included no word about the various slip covers of novels which bear words of praise from Mr. Cabell. I do not list the catalogue of unpublished books by Benjamin de Casseres, or the catalogues of published books by any number of writers, which contain what publishers shyly call "expressions of opinion" from Mr. Cabell. I do not mention the by no means inconsiderable list of newspapers which once published Mr. Cabell's contribution to a symposium upon "Why People Should Own and Read Books," and his contribution to that other symposium, later reprinted, I am told, in pamphlet form and distributed by Marshall Field & Company of Chicago, upon "The Books I Read as a Child." A scarce item, this, they tell me.

Then, too, I am guilty of ignoring the December, 1923, issue of Mr. Percy Beach's entertaining Book Notes (pp. 8, unbound: Indianapolis: Beach's Bookshop, 1923) on the front page of which appears a facsimile reproduction of a Cabell acrostic to Mr. George T. Keating.

But far more grave, it may be, is the omission from the tale of a Report on a Collection of Hemiptera-Heteroptera from South Dakota by H. M. Parshley, Sc. D., South Dakota State College, (Technical Bulletin No. 2, Smith

College, Northampton, Mass., 1922).   For here on page 19 you will find described *Rhagovelia oriander* of the family *Velidae*, which, a footnote informs the reader, derives its name from *Oriander the Swimmer* in *Figures of Earth*.   Here in very truth is a rare sample of Mr. Cabell's creative work.   For the first Oriander was no other than the compositor whose name appeared upon the galley proofs of *Domnei*: and Cabell, noting and liking the name, made its bearer a god, from which state he was transformed by Mr. Parshley into a water-bug. . . To a committee of collectors I leave the determination of whether this monograph is, or is not, an authentic Cabell item.   To that committee, also, I am ready to leave the discovery of any additional Cabell items of which I and the author have no present cognizance.

One word more: Today, for the first time, I have read — with admiration at the spectacle of a style so completely perfected that it may take form without the admixture of an alien element — Mr. Cabell's foreword, *About These Books*. To some the almost disquieting similarity in the matter of our observations may seem worthy of comment; and it may even appear obligatory upon either the author or his bibliographer to be somewhat more communicative than, say, a trust magnate at a Senate inquiry.   To this omission also I have given thought, but I must content myself with the information that a few pages on begins the record. Beyond this, I, too, although so much less magnificently, have nothing to say about these books.

GUY HOLT

New York,
February 13, 1924

FIRST EDITIONS

(1)

THE EAGLE'S SHADOW

Published 4 October 1904

THE / EAGLE'S SHADOW / by / James Branch Cabell / Illustrated by Will Grefé / Decorated by Blanche Ostertag / (*Design*) / New York / Doubleday, Page & Company / 1904 /

> COLLATION: — pp. xiv+258, (together with a frontispiece and seven pages of illustrations) consisting of blank leaf; (i) Half-title: (*decoration*) The / Eagle's Shadow; verso: blank; (insert) Frontispiece: "Margaret'; (iii) Title-page (as above); verso: (*decoration*) / Copyright, 1904, by / The Curtis Publishing Company / Copyright, 1904, by / Doubleday, Page & Company / Published, October, 1904 / An abridged version of this story appeared serially in The Saturday Evening Post / during the summer of 1904. The novel is here given in its entirety / as originally conceived by the author / (v) Dedication: (*decoration*) To / M. L. P. B. / In trust that the enterprise may be judged / less by the merits of its factor than / by those of its patron /; verso: blank; vii-viii Contents; (ix-x) The Characters; (xi) List of Illustrations; verso: blank; (1) Fly-leaf (as before); verso: blank; 3-256 text. (257-258) blank.

Crown octavo 8×5¼: issued in red cloth lettered in gold, all edges cut; pictorial end-papers, title and preliminary pages printed in green. Front cover: *The / Eagle's Shadow /* (design in white and gold) / *James Branch Cabell /.* Backbone: *The / Eagle's / Shadow / Cabell /* (design in white and gold) / *Doubleday / Page & Co.* In the first state alone, the dedication (p. v) reads as above [*To / M. L. P. B. / In trust that the enterprise may be judged / less by the merits of its factor than / by those of its patron /*]. In the second state, the first two lines are altered to read: *To / Martha Louise Branch /.* In each of these states, the frontispiece, "Margaret' (second quotation mark defective), represents a girl seated. In the third state, this frontispiece was changed for a drawing of a girl standing, and the title correctly given as "Margaret." In the fourth state, the pictorial endpapers were omitted, and in the fifth white substituted for gold in the cover stamping.

A small English edition, from imported sheets in the first state, bound in green cloth with blue and black stamping and gilt lettering, was issued in the autumn of 1904, by Wm. Heinemann.

(2)

THE LINE OF LOVE

Published 28 September 1905

THE LINE OF LOVE / by / James Branch Cabell / Illustrated in color by / Howard Pyle / "*Ludit amor sensus, oculos perstringit, et aufert / Libertatem animi, mira nos fascinat arte. / Credo aliquis dæmon subiens præcordia flammam / Concitat, et raptam tollit de cardine mentem"* / (*publishers' device*) / New York and London / Harper & Brothers / Publishers : : MCMV /.

COLLATION: — pp. xii+292 (together with one page frontispiece and nine pages of illustrations in color), consisting of: Frontispiece; (i) Title-page (as above); verso: Copyright, 1905, by Harper & Brothers. / (*a line*) / All rights reserved. / Published September, 1905. / (The preceding enclosed in rules.) (iii) Dedication page: To / Robert Gamble Cabell / (1809-1889) / "He loved chivalrye, / Trouthe and honour, fredom and curteisye. / And of his port as meek as is a mayde, / He never yet no vileinye ne sayde / In al his lyf, unto no maner wight. / He was a verray parfit gentil knyght" / verso: blank; (v) Contents; verso: blank; (vii) List of Illustrations; verso: blank; ix-(xii), Epistle Dedicatory; (1) Divisional Half-title: 1 / April 14, 1355—October 23, 1356 / "D'aquest segle flac, plen de marrimen, / S'amor s'en vai, son joi teinh mensongier" /; verso: blank; (3)-(292), text.

Demy octavo 9×6: issued in light green cloth, gilt lettering, white ornamentation, and colored oval paster on front cover. Gilt top, otherwise untrimmed. Front cover: *The Line Of Love* / (oval paster, to left) / *James Branch Cabell.* / Backbone: *The / Line / of / Love / J. B. / Cabell / Harpers /* . The book was later issued in a variety of less expensive bindings: the first binding is distinguishable by the fact that it alone has gilt lettering. All issues have pictorial end-papers and page borderings printed in orange.

CONTENTS: Epistle Dedicatory; The Episode Called Adhelmar at Puysange; The Episode Called Love-Letters of

Falstaff; The Episode Called "Sweet Adelais"; The Episode Called In Necessity's Mortar; The Episode Called The Conspiracy of Arnaye; The Episode Called The Castle of Content; The Episode Called In Ursula's Garden; Envoi.

(3)

BRANCHIANA

Published 10 October 1907

BRANCHIANA / Being a Partial Account of / The Branch Family in Virginia / by / James Branch Cabell / "*Hæc est / Vita solutorum misera ambitione gravique.*" / (*fleur-de-lis*) / Printed by / Whittet & Shepperson, / Richmond, Va. /

> COLLATION: — pp. iv (unnumbered)+180 (together with a frontispiece and eight pages of illustrations) consisting of: (i) This edition of Branchiana is limited / to one hundred and forty-seven / copies, of which this copy is number — / [*author's signature*]; verso: blank; Frontispiece, Tho. Branch [*reproduction of signature*]; (iii) Title-page (as above); verso: blank; (1) (Dedication) To / John Patteson Branch / this volume is with a double fitness dedicated, as being both / the first to suggest its compilation and the most / eminent living member of the family / which it commemorates. /; verso: blank; (3) Contents; verso: blank; (5) Half-title; The Compiler's Foreword; verso: blank; 7-177, text; (178) blank; (179) Errata; (180) blank.

Demy octavo 9⅝×6¼: issued in green or red cloth, gilt lettering, gilt top, otherwise untrimmed. Front cover:

Branchiana / (armorial design in lower right hand corner). Backbone: *Branchiana* / (fleuron) / *James* / *Branch* / *Cabell* /. White end papers.

The first edition consists of 147 numbered and signed copies. Thirty copies were later bound up in buff cloth, $9\frac{3}{4}\times6\frac{1}{4}$. This second binding lacks all portraits except the frontispiece, and has two gilt lines at the top and again at the bottom of backbone.

(4)

GALLANTRY

Published 10 October 1907

GALLANTRY / An Eighteenth Century Dizain / in Ten Comedies, with / an Afterpiece / By / James Branch Cabell / *"Sumite materiam vestris, qui scribitis, æquam / Viribus, et versate diu, quid ferre recusent, / Quid valeant umeri."* / Illustrated in Color / by Howard Pyle / (*publishers' device*) / New York and London / Harper & Brothers Publishers / 1907 /.

COLLATION: — pp. x (unnumbered)+334, (together with a frontispiece and 3 pages of illustrations) consisting of: Insert Frontispiece. (i) Title-page (as above), verso: Copyright, 1907, by Harper & Brothers / (*a line*) / All rights reserved. / Published October, 1907. / (iii) Dedication page: To the Memory of / Midshipman James R. Branch / Killed at Annapolis, November 5, 1905 / this volume, since it treats of gallantry, / is dedicated, as both in life and death / an exponent of the word's true / and highest meaning / (*fleuret*) / "A brutish man knoweth not, neither doth a fool / understand this. . . . Shall the throne of iniquity / have fellowship with Thee, which frameth mischief / by a law?" /; verso: blank; (v) Foreword (untitled — containing acknowledgements of the previous appearance of a portion of the book's contents); verso: blank; (vii) Contents; verso: blank; (ix) List of Illustrations; verso: blank; (1) Half-title: The Epistle Dedicatory; (2) blank; 3-334: text.

Demy 8vo 9×6: issued in silver gray cloth, with gilt lettering and silver and white ornamentation. Gilt top, otherwise untrimmed. Front cover: *Gallantry / James Branch Cabell /*. Backbone: *Gallantry / Cabell / Harpers /*. Later bindings omit the gilt. All states contain pictorial end-papers, and a title-page design and four illustrations (tipped in) by Howard Pyle.

CONTENTS: The Epistle Dedicatory; The Prologue; Simon's Hour; Love at Martinmas; The Casual Honeymoon; The Rhyme to Porringer; Actors All; April's Message; In the Second April; Heart of Gold; The Scapegoats; The Ducal Audience; Love's Alumni; The Epilogue.

(5)

THE CORDS OF VANITY

Published 11 March 1909

THE CORDS OF VANITY / By / James Branch Cabell / (*publishers' device*) / New York / Doubleday, Page & Company / 1909 /.

COLLATION: — pp. xx+344 (together with a front-

ispiece in color, by C. Coles Phillips) consisting of: (i) Half-title: The Cords of Vanity;
verso: blank; Insert, Frontispiece: "I Adored
Within These Four Years Precisely a Dozen Girls, /
and . . . Wrote Verses of Them." / (iii) Title-
page, (as above): verso: All rights reserved, including
that of Translation / into Foreign Languages, including the Scandinavian / Copyright, 1909, by Doubleday,
Page & Company / Published, March, 1909 / (v)
Dedication page: To / Gabrielle Brooke Moncure /
Plus sapit vulgus, quia tantum, quantum opus est,
sapit. /; verso: blank; (vii) "His has been the Summer
Air, and the / Sunshine, and the Flowers; and Gentle
/ Ears have listened to Him, and Gentle / Eyes have
been upon Him. Let others eat / His Honey that
please, so that he has had / his Morsel and his
Song." /; verso: blank; ix-x Contents: xi-xx, Prologue;
(1) Half-title; The Cords of Vanity; verso: blank;
3-341, text.   (342-344) blank.

Crown octavo $7\frac{3}{4} \times 5$; issued in red ribbed cloth lettered
in white, all edges cut. Front cover: *Cords / of / Vanity / James Branch Cabell /*. Backbone: *Cords / of /
Vanity / Cabell / Doubleday / Page & Co. /* Later
bindings than the first restore the omitted "The" of the
book's title, upon both cover and backbone. White end
papers. On front cover Cords of Vanity is enclosed in
single white rule.

A small English edition, from imported sheets, was issued in the spring of 1909, by Wm. Heinemann.

(6)

CHIVALRY

Published 21 October 1909

CHIVALRY / By / James Branch Cabell / *"And I, according to my copy, and / after the simple cunning that God hath / sent to me, have down set this in print, / io the intent that noble men may see and / learn the noble acts of chivalry."* / Illustrated / (*publishers' device*) / New York and London / Harper & Brothers Publishers / 1909 /.

COLLATION : — pp. (xii) +226 (together with twelve pages of illustrations), consisting of blank leaf; Frontispiece: Painting by Howard Pyle / "'I sing of Death'" /; (i) Title-page: as above; verso: Copyright, 1909, by Harper & Brothers. / (*A line*) / All rights reserved. / Published October, 1909. / (The preceding enclosed in rules); (iii) Dedication: To / Anne Branch Cabell / (*fleuret*) / "Ainsi à vous, Madame, à ma très haulte et / très noble dame, à qui j'ayme à devoir / attachement et obéissance, / j' envoye ce livret." / (*fleuret*) /; verso: blank; v-vii, Precautional; verso: blank; (ix) Contents; verso: blank; (xi) List of Illustrations; verso: blank; (1) The Prologue / "Afin que les entreprises honorables et les nobles aven- / tures et faicts d'armes soyent noblement enregistrés et con- / servés, je vais traiter et raconter et inventer ung galimatias." / Verso: The Dizain of Queens of that Noble Maker in the / French Tongue, Messire, Nicolas De Caen, Dedicated / To the Most Illustrious Isabella of Portugal, of / the House of the Indomitable Alfonso Henriques, / and Duchess Dowager of Burgundy. Here begins / in Auspicious wise the Prologue. /; 3-224, text; (225-226) blank.

Demy 8vo 8⅞×5¾: issued in red cloth, with gilt lettering and green and white ornamentation. The design of the binding is uniform with that of the first printed version of Gallantry. Gilt top, otherwise untrimmed. Front cover: *Chivalry / James Branch Cabell /*. Backbone: *Chivalry / Cabell / Harpers /*. Later bindings omit the gilt. Early bindings contain colored end-papers, a title-page design and nine illustrations in color (including the frontispiece) by Howard Pyle, two illustrations in color by William Hurd Lawrence, and one illustration in color by Elizabeth Shippen Green.

Contents: Precautional; The Prologue; The Story of the Sestina; The Story of the Tenson; The Story of the Rat-Trap; The Story of the Choices; The Story of the Housewife; The Story of the Satraps; The Story of the Heritage; The Story of the Scabbard; The Story of the Navarrese; The Story of the Fox-Brush; The Epilogue.

(7)

BRANCH OF ABINGDON

Published 27 December 1911

Branch of Abingdon / Being a Partial Account of / The Ancestry of Christopher Branch of / "Arrowhat-tocks" and "Kingsland," in / Henrico County, and the Founder of / the Branch Family in Virginia / by / James Branch Cabell / (*fleuron*) / *"Volentem proelia me loqui / Victas et urbis increpuit lyra."* / (fleuron) / Printed by / Wm. Ellis Jones' Sons, Inc. / Richmond, Va. /

COLLATION: — pp. vi (unnumbered)+136 (together with a frontispiece and nine pages of illustrations), consisting of: (i-ii), blank; (iii) Half-title: Branch of Abingdon; verso: blank; (v) Books by Mr. Cabell (Followed by a list, the whole enclosed in rules); verso: blank; Frontispiece, (caption on facing tissue in red) Facsimile Page from The Cartulary of the / Fraternity of the Holy Cross; (1) Title-page (as above); verso: Copyright, 1911, by James Branch Cabell. / All rights reserved. / Published December, 1911. / (The preceding enclosed in rules) (3) Dedication: To / James Ransom Branch / as the lineal male representative of / Richard Branch of Abingdon / in the twelfth generation /; verso: blank; (5) Contents; verso: blank; (7) Illustrations; verso: blank; (9) Half-title: The Compiler's Foreword; verso: blank; (11) text of The Compiler's Foreword; verso: blank; (13) Fly-leaf: Of the Branches in General; verso: blank; 15-126, text; (127) Other Books by Mr. Cabell; verso: blank; (129-134, unnumbered) Advertising pages; (135-136) blank.

Demy octavo $9\frac{3}{4} \times 6\frac{1}{4}$: issued in green cloth, gilt lettering, gilt top, otherwise untrimmed. Front cover: *Branch of Abingdon* / (armorial design in lower right hand corner). Backbone: (two lines) / Branch / of / Abingdon / (fleuron) / *James / Branch / Cabell / Wm. Ellis Jones' / Sons, Inc. / Publishers.* / (two lines). / White end papers.

This edition consisted of 100 signed and numbered copies, with extra fly-leaf, and of 100 copies as above.

(Kingsland Edition)

BRANCH OF ABINGDON / Being a Partial Account of / The Branch Family in England / by / James Branch

Cabell / (*fleuron*) / The Kingsland Edition / (*fleuron*) / "*Volentem proelia me loqui / Victas et urbis increpuit lyra.*" / (*fleuron*) / Wm. Ellis Jones' Sons / Richmond, — Virginia / MDCCCCXI /.

Demy octavo 9¾×6¼: issued in red morocco, with silk end-papers. The cover design is as above, but the backbone lacks the printer's name, and has a single line at top. The advertising pages at back are omitted. This Kingsland edition, printed on Japan vellum paper, was limited to fifteen signed and numbered copies, of which only ten were actually made, these being numbered 1, 2, 3, 4, 5, 6, 11, 12, 14, and 15. In copies 11, 12, 14, and 15, the seventh line of page 114 was reset, the word "Mercia" being substituted for "Chester."

All copies of Branch of Abingdon were issued simultaneously, except copies 11, 12, 14 and 15 of the Kingsland Edition. The error on page 114 was noted before the type was taken down, correction made, and the four copies completed.

(8)

THE SOUL OF MELICENT

Published September 1913

THE SOUL OF / MELICENT / by / James Branch Cabell / Illustrated in Colour by / Howard Pyle / (*publisher's device*) / New York / Frederick A. Stokes Company / Publishers /.

COLLATION: — pp. viii (unnumbered)+216 (together with a frontispiece and three pages of illustrations in color, by Howard Pyle), consisting of p. (i) Half-title: (*a line*) / The Soul of Melicent / (*a line*) ; verso: Other books by Mr. Cabell / (followed by a list, the whole enclosed in rules) ; Frontispiece: "Demetrios wrenched the sword from its scabbard."; (iii) Title-page: as above, verso: Copyright, 1913, by / Frederick A. Stokes Company / Copyright, 1908, 1911, by / Harper & Brothers / (*a line*) / All rights reserved / (Below, in decorative box) September, 1913 /; (v) Dedication page: To / Sarah Read McAdams / in Gratitude and Affection /; verso: Fourteen lines of verse; (vii-viii) : Contents; (1) Half-title: Part One / Perion / (followed by eight lines of verse); verso: blank; pp. 3-213, text; verso of 213, blank; 215-216, Bibliography.

Post octavo $8\frac{3}{4}\times5\frac{1}{2}$: issued in dark blue cloth lettered in gold, all edges cut. Front cover: *The Soul of Melicent* / (pictorial paster) / (design) *James Branch Cabell* (design) / *Illustrated by Howard Pyle* /. Backbone: *The Soul* / *of* / *Melicent* / (a line) / *Cabell* / *Stokes* /. White end papers.

Later bindings of this book were in black cloth. A few copies of the earliest printed show p. ii (devoted to a list of Other Books by Mr. Cabell) as blank.

(9)

THE RIVET IN GRANDFATHER'S NECK

Published 13 October 1915

THE RIVET / IN GRANDFATHER'S / NECK / A Comedy of Limitations / by / James Branch Cabell / "*To this*

*new South, who values her high / past, in chief, as fit
foundation of that edifice / whereon she labors day by
day, and with / augmenting strokes."* / New York /
Robert M. McBride & Company / 1915 /.

> COLLATION: — pp. 368 (the first twelve unnumber-
> ed), consisting of: (1) Half-title: The Rivet in /
> Grandfather's Neck; verso: Books by Mr. Cabell / (*a
> line*) / (followed by a list of books, the whole en-
> closed in rules); (3) Title-page: as above; verso:
> Copyright, 1915, by / Robert M. McBride & Co.
> / (*a line*) / Published October, 1915 /; (5) Dedi-
> cation page: To / Priscilla Bradley Cabell / (fol-
> lowed by dedicatory sonnet) /; verso: blank ; (7)
> Contents; verso: blank; (9) Note (untitled, being
> a quotation from Hans Andersen's tale *The Shepherd-
> ess and the Chimney-Sweep*); verso: blank; (11)
> Half-title; (*two lines*) / Part I / Propinquity / (*a
> line*) / verso: (Contains a sonnet) / Paul Verville.
> Nascitur. /; 13-368 text.

Crown octavo $7\frac{7}{8} \times 5$: brown cloth, gilt lettering, all
edges trimmed. Front cover: *The Rivet in / Grand-
father's / Neck* / (design of seated Chinese figure) /
James Branch Cabell / (the whole enclosed in gilt rule).
Backbone: *The Rivet / in / Grand- / fathers / Neck* /
(a line) / *Cabell / McBride* /. White end papers. It
will be noted that the apostrophe in "Grandfather's"
is lacking on backbone of the first three printings.
With the third printing (March 1920) the book was
issued in the Kalki binding, of brown cloth, in which
the front cover is unstamped except in the lower right
hand corner, which displays in gilt the Kalki device —

within a circle, upon an heraldic wreath a rampant but bridled stallion.

This novel has never been revised, but a number of verbal changes were made in the text of the fifth printing, October 1922.

A small English edition from imported sheets was issued in the autumn of 1915, by McBride, Nast & Company, Ltd. In some copies of this the binding is similar to the first American edition; in others the Chinese figure is omitted, the lettering upon front cover is in black, and the binding of blue-gray cloth.

(10)

THE MAJORS AND THEIR MARRIAGES
Published 13 December 1915

THE MAJORS AND / THEIR MARRIAGES / by / James Branch Cabell / With Collateral Accounts of the Allied / Families of Aston, Ballard, Christian, / Dancy, Hart- / well, Hubard, Macon, Mar- / able, Mason, Patteson, Piersey, Seawell, / Stephens, Waddill, and Others. / (*device*) / "*Fortuna non mutat genus*" / (*device*) / The W. C. Hill Printing Co., / Richmond, Va. /

COLLATION: — pp. 188, consisting of: (1) (*Decoration*) / Books by Mr. Cabell / (Followed by a list of books, and a decoration, the whole enclosed in rules); verso: blank; (3) This, the Burlington Edition of / "The Majors and their Marriages," / is Limited to One Hundred Copies, / of which this Book is Number —— / (Author's Signature); verso: blank; (5)

Title-page (as above); verso: Copyright, December, 1915, / By / James Branch Cabell. /; (7) Dedication: To / Ballard Hartwell Cabell / In Commemoration of His Christening /; verso: blank; (9-10) Acknowledgement at Large; (11) Contents; verso: blank: 13-188, text.

Demy octavo $9\frac{3}{4}\times6\frac{1}{8}$: issued in green cloth, gilt lettering, top trimmed, otherwise uncut.   Front cover: *The Majors and / Their Marriages / James / Branch / Cabell /* (armorial design to lower left hand corner).   Backbone: (two lines) / *The Majors / and Their / Marriages /* (ornament) / *Cabell / W. C. Hill Printing / Company / Richmond, Va. /* (two lines).

This is the numbered and signed Burlington edition of 100 copies.   At the same time was issued the Roxbury edition of 200 unnumbered and unsigned copies. $9\frac{1}{2}\times6\frac{1}{4}$: in blue-gray or buff paper, black lettering, top trimmed, otherwise uncut.   Front cover: *The Majors and / Their Marriages / The Roxbury Edition / Price, $2.50 /* (ornament) / *This book can also be procured in the cloth- / bound Burlington Edition, at $3.50 /* Backbone lettered vertically: *The Majors and Their Marriages /.*   188 pp. and a blank leaf.

(11)

THE CERTAIN HOUR

Published 4 November 1916

The / Certain Hour / (Dizain des Poëtes) / By / James Branch Cabell / *"Criticism, whatever may be its pretensions, never / does more than to define the impression which / is made upon it at a certain moment by a work / wherein the writer himself noted the impression / of the world which he received at a certain hour."* / New York / Robert M. McBride & Company / 1916 /.

COLLATION: — pp. 256, consisting of: (1) Half-title: The Certain Hour; verso: Books by Mr. Cabell / (*a line*) / (Followed by a list of books, the whole enclosed in rules); (3) Title-page as above; verso: Copyright, 1916, by Robert M. McBride & Co. / Copyright, 1915, by McBride, Nast & Co. / Copyright, 1914, by The Sewanee Review Quarterly / Copyright, 1913, by John Adams Thayer Corporation / Copyright, 1912, by Argonaut Publishing Company / Copyright, 1911, by Red Book Corporation / Copyright, 1909, by Harper and Brothers /; (5) Dedication page: To / Robert Gamble Cabell II / In Dedication of The Certain Hour / Sad hours and glad hours, and all hours pass over; / One thing unshaken stays: / Life, that hath Death for spouse, hath Chance for lover; / Whereby decays / Each thing save one thing: — mid this strife diurnal / Of hourly change begot, / Love that is God-born, bides as God eternal, / And changes not;— / Nor means a tinseled dream pursuing lovers / Find altered by-and-bye, / When, with possession, time anon discovers / Trapped dreams must die, — / For he that visions God, of mankind gathers / One manlike trait alone, / And reverently imputes to Him a father's / Love for his son. /; verso: blank; (7) Contents; verso: blank; 9-253, text; 254-256 blank.

Crown octavo $7\frac{1}{8}\times5$: brown cloth, gilt lettering, all edges trimmed. Front cover: *The / Certain / Hour / James Branch Cabell /.* Backbone: *The / Certain /*

Hour / (a line) / *Cabell* / *McBride* /.   White end papers.

The first printing of this book was from type: the second and third printings are easily distinguishable as zinced, and are in the Kalki binding.

CONTENTS: "Ballad of the Double-Soul"; Auctorial Induction; Belhs Cavaliers; Balthazar's Daughter; Judith's Creed; Concerning Corinna; Olivia's Pottage; A Brown Woman; Pro Honoria; The Irresistible Ogle; A Princess of Grub Street; The Lady of All Our Dreams; "Ballad of Plagiary."

A small English edition, from imported sheets, was issued in the autumn of 1916, by McBride, Nast & Company.

(12)

FROM THE HIDDEN WAY

Published 18 November 1916

FROM THE / HIDDEN WAY / Being Seventy-Five / Adaptations in Verse / by / James Branch Cabell / (*two lines*) / *"Tell me now in what hidden way* / *is Lady Flora, the lovely Roman?* / *Where's Hipparchia? where is Thais?"* / (*two lines*) / New York / Robert M. McBride & Co. / 1916 /.

COLLATION:— pp. (ii)+190, consisting of: (i) blank; verso, Books by Mr. Cabell / (*a double line*) / (followed by a list of books, the whole enclosed in double rules); (1) Title-page: as above; verso: Copyright, 1916, / By Robert M. McBride &

Co. /; (3) Dedication page: To / Beverley Bland Munford / (31 May 1910) / "Most blithe and sage and gentle, and most brave! / O true clear heart, so quick to wake and war / Against despondency, lest questioning mar / One hour of living, or foiled hopes enslave / And sour another's living! not to the grave / Do we commit you, — we that, watching, are / As men at twilight noting which bright star / Is leaped at, missed, clutched, swallowed by which wave. / "The star is gone? — So be it. It will rise / Elsewhere, and undiminished. Even thus / We know that instantly in Paradise — / Yea, in the inmost court of Heaven's house, — / A gentleman to God lifts those brave eyes / Which yesterday made life more brave for us." /; verso: blank; pp. 5-8 Contents; (9) Half-title: (*a line*) / Apologia Auctoris / "Vous entendez bien jon-cherie?" / (*a double line*) /; verso: blank; 11-187, text; 188-190 blank.

Crown octavo 7⅝×5: brown cloth, gilt lettering, all edges trimmed. Front cover: *From the / Hidden / Way* (ornament) / *James / Branch / Cabell* /. Backbone: *From / the / Hidden / Way* / (a line) / *Cabell / McBride* / White end papers. Of this book only 620 copies were printed, from type.

The first state, which consisted of 245 copies, was bound as above without the dropped *c* in McBride on the backbone underlined, and is less tall, by ¼ inch, than later issues. In the second state (1920) of 99 copies the *c* was raised and underlined; the third state (1920) of 176 copies was bound in the correct shade of brown cloth — unlike the first two which were nearly wine-colored — but bore the original design; the fourth (1921) of 100 copies was in the Kalki binding.

(13)

THE CREAM OF THE JEST

Published 27 September 1917

THE / CREAM / OF THE / JEST / (*a line*) / A Comedy of Evasions / (*a line*) / by / James Branch Cabell / "*Le-pays où je voulais aller, tu m'y as mené / en songe, cette nuit, et tu étais belle . . . / ah! que tu étais belle! . . . Mais, comme / je n'ai aimé que ton ombre, tu me dispen- / seras, chère tête, de remercier ta réalité.*" / New York / Robert M. McBride & Company / 1917 /.

COLLATION: — pp. xvi+280, consisting of: (i) Half-title: The / Cream / of / the / Jest /; verso: blank; (ii) Books by Mr. Cabell / (followed by a list of books, printed in Italics and not enclosed in rules); verso: reproduction of cryptogrammatic seal; (v) Title-page (as above); verso: Copyright, 1917, by / Robert M. McBride & Co. / (*a line*) / (*a line*) / Published September 1917 /; (vii) Dedication: To / Louisa Nelson / "At me ab amore tuo diducet / nulla senectus." /; verso: blank; (ix) Contents; verso: (Contents continued); (xi) (Contents concluded); verso: blank; xiii-xv: Preface; verso: blank; (1) Half-title: Book First / (*a line*) / "Give place, fair ladies, and begone, / Ere pride hath had a fall! / For here at hand approacheth one / Whose grace doth stain you all. / "Ettarre is well compared / Unto the Phoenix kind, / Whose like was never seen or heard / That any man can find." /; verso: blank; 3-280, text.

Crown octavo 7¾×5⅛: brown cloth, gilt lettering, top trimmed, otherwise uncut. Front cover: *The / Cream / of the / Jest / James / Branch / Cabell /*. Backbone: *The / Cream / of the / Jest* / (small square) / *Cabell /*

McBride /.   (Lettering on front cover in brown against two squares of gilt).   White end papers.

The first printing of this book was from type: the second, third, and fourth printings are easily distinguishable as zinced, and are in the Kalki binding.

(14)
BEYOND LIFE

Published 18 January 1919

BEYOND / LIFE / (*a line*) / *Dizain des Demiurges* / (*a line*) / by / James Branch Cabell / "*Many a man lives a burden to the earth*: / *but a good book is the precious life-blood of a* / *master-spirit, embalmed and treasured up on pur-* / *pose to a life beyond life.*" / New York / Robert M. McBride & Company / 1919 /.

COLLATION: — pp.   (viii)+368,   consisting   of   p. (i) Half-title: Beyond Life; verso: Books by Mr. Cabell [followed by a list of books, the whole en- closed in double rules]; (iii) Title-page: as above; verso: Copyright 1919 / By / Robert M. McBride & Company / (*a line*) / Printed in The United States of America / (*a line*) / Published January, 1919. /; (v) Dedication: (*two lines*) / To / Guy Holt / Garrulity again begets / Unconscionable dreadful debts . . . / You that have piped to-day must dance; / Herein be- holding maintenance / Of arguments about Romance / (Like fountains falling whence they spring) / To you revert its eddying. / (*two lines*) /; verso: blank; (vii) Contents; verso: blank; (1) Half-title: 1 / We Aproach; verso: [Several lines of a quotation from

Ashtaroth's Lacky]; 3-358, text; 359, Some Other Books by Mr. Cabell] / (with Tributes of the Press) / [Quotation]; 360-366, Reviews of other books by Mr. Cabell; 367-368 blank.

Crown octavo $7\frac{9}{16}\times5$: brown cloth, gilt lettering, all edges trimmed. Some few of the earliest issues were, by accident, bound in a very dark cloth, "Italian chocolate," which approaches black. Front cover: *Beyond Life / James Branch Cabell /*. Backbone: *Beyond / Life / (a line) / Cabell / McBride /*. White end papers.

There was a second printing in 1919, wherein upon the title-page "Demiurges" is corrected to "Démiurges" and numerals are omitted from the flyleaves.

Beyond Life was in 1923 included in The Modern Library, as published by Boni & Liveright, New York: pp. xxii+358. This is a reprint from the original plates, omitting pp. 359-366, and with the addition of an Introduction by Guy Holt, which in The Modern Library edition composes pp. ix-xix.

(15)

JURGEN

Published 27 September 1919

JURGEN / (*a line broken by the lower portion of the "G"*) / A Comedy of Justice / (*a line*) / By / James Branch Cabell / "Of JURGEN eke they maken mencioun, / That of an old wyf gat his youthe agoon, / And gat himselfe a shirte as bright as fyre / Wherein to jape,

yet gat not his desire / In any countrie ne condicioun." /
New York / Robert M. McBride & Co. / 1919 /.

> COLLATION: — pp. (viii)+368 consisting of (i) Half-
> title: Jurgen; verso: Books by Mr. Cabell [followed
> by a list of books, the whole enclosed in rules]; (iii)
> Title-page: as above; verso: Copyright, 1919, by /
> Robert M. McBride & Co. / (*a line*) / Printed in /
> The United States of America / (*a line*) / Published
> August, 1919 /; (v) Dedication: To / Burton Rascoe
> / Before each tarradiddle / Uncowed by sciolists, / Ro-
> buster persons twiddle / Tremendously big fists. /
> "Our gods are good," they tell us; / "Nor will our
> gods defer / Remission of rude fellows' / Ability to
> err." / So this, your Jurgen, travels / Content to
> compromise / Ordainments none unravels / Explicitly
> . . . and sighs /; verso [Three quotations, from, re-
> spectively, Philip Borsdale, E. Noel Codman, and
> John Frederick Lewistam]; (vii-viii) Contents; (1)
> Divisional half-title: (*A line*) / A Foreword / "Nescio
> quid certè est: et Hylax in limine latrat." / (*a line*) /;
> verso: blank; (3-5) A Foreword: Which Asserts Noth-
> ing [with text]; (6) blank; (7) Divisional half-title:
> (*A line*) / Jurgen / . . . amara lento temperet risu
> / (*a line*) /; (8) blank; 9-368, text.

Crown 8vo $7\frac{7}{8}+5\frac{1}{8}$: brown cloth, gilt lettering, top
trimmed, otherwise uncut.   Front cover: *Jurgen* / (within lower portion of the "g") *James* / *Branch* / *Cabell* /.
Backbone: *Jurgen* / (a line) / *Cabell* / *McBride* /.
White end papers.

The copyright page, erroneously, states the book to have
been published in August 1919.   A second printing was
issued November 1919, in all respects identical with the
first, except that the first printing measures $1\frac{3}{8}$ inches

across the top, in all, and the second is about ¼ of an inch
thicker.   The third printing, December 1919, was the first
of Mr. Cabell's books to be issued in the Kalki binding.
In the eighth printing the Foreword was increased by
four pages (3-6, unnumbered) of additional matter, so as
to include *The Judging of Jurgen.*

An English edition, with illustrations and decorations by
Frank C. Papé, and an introduction by Hugh Walpole,
was issued by John Lane, November, 1921.   An illus-
trated edition was also issued by Robert M. McBride &
Co. in December, 1923, with twelve drawings by Ray F.
Coyle.

(16)

THE CORDS OF VANITY

Revised version, published 28 September 1920

The / Cords of Vanity / (*a broken line*) / A Comedy
of Shirking / (*a line*) / by / James Branch Cabell /
With an introduction by Wilson Follett / "*Woe unto
them that draw iniquity with cords / of vanity! . . .
their root shall be as rottenness / and their blossom shall
go up as dust.*" / New York / Robert M. McBride &
Co. / 1920 /.

> Collation : — pp. (xvi) + 330, consisting of (i) Half-
> title : The Cords of Vanity; verso : Books by Mr. Ca-
> bell [followed by a list of books, the whole enclosed
> in rules] ; (iii) Title-page : as above; verso : Copyright,
> 1909, by Doubleday, Page & Co. / Copyright, 1918,
> by James Branch Cabell. / Revised Edition, Copyright,

1920, by / James Branch Cabell. / Printed in the United States of America / Published 1920; (v) Dedication: (as on p. (v) of the original edition); verso: blank; (vii) Divisional Half-title: (*a line*) / An Introduction / by / Wilson Follett / (*a line*); verso: blank; (ix-xiv) text of introduction; (xv), Contents; verso: blank; (1) Divisional Half-title: (*a line*) / The Prologue / "In the house and garden of his dream he saw a child mov- / ing, and could divide the main streams at least of the winds / that had played on him, and study so the first stage in that / mental journey." / (*a line*) /; (2) blank; 3-11, text of Prologue; (12) blank; (13) Divisional Half-title: (*a line*) / The Cords of Vanity / [followed by passage quoted on p. (vii) of original edition]; (14) blank; 15-330, text.

Crown 8vo 7¾×5: brown cloth, gilt, top trimmed, otherwise uncut. Front cover: Kalki device, in lower left hand corner. Backbone: *The / Cords / of / Vanity / Cabell / McBride /*. White end papers.

The revised text, which in its first printing has a special value as a thesaurus of all possible typographical errors, is augmented by an introduction by Wilson Follett (pp. ix-xiv).

(17)

THE JUDGING OF JURGEN

Published October 1920

THE JUDGING OF JURGEN / By / James Branch Cabell / (*dolphin and anchor design*) / Chicago / The Bookfellows / 1920 /.

Collation: — pp. 16 (the first 8 unnumbered) consisting of p. (1): Half-title: The Judging of Jurgen; verso: blank; (3) Title-page: as above; verso: The Judging of Jurgen, by James Branch Cabell, Book-fellow / No. 513, is reprinted by permission from the New York / Tribune.   Acknowledgement is also made to Vincent Starrett, / Bookfellow No. 8. / This is the Bookly Joy for October, 1920; (5) J. B. C.: In Gratitude / (followed by a sonnet, the initial in red) / — Vincent Starrett; verso: blank; (7) In this, as in every other fable / I have written about Jurgen, I have / endeavored to write that wherein / each man will find what his nature / enables him to see. / James Branch Cabell / 29 May 1920 / (The preceding is printed in a reproduction of the author's handwriting); verso: blank; pp. 9-14, text; (15-16) blank.

Thin demy 8vo 8½×5¾: pamphlet, green, blue, brown or buff paper covers, with cord binding.   Front cover: (on white paper label) *The Judging of Jurgen / By James Branch Cabell /.*

The large paper edition of six copies is 11½×8⅝, bound in brown boards, dark red cloth back, with white paper label on front cover.

The text of this pamphlet was worked into the thirty-second chapter of the English edition of *Jurgen*, and in the American edition was, with the eighth printing, added to the Foreword.

(18)

DOMNEI

Revised version of The Soul of Melicent, published 22
October 1920

DOMNEI / A Comedy of Woman-Worship / By / James
Branch Cabell / (*a line*) / "*En cor gentil domnei per
mort no passa.*" / (*a line*) / New York / Robert M.
McBride & Co. / 1920 /.

COLLATION:— pp. viii+218, consisting of a blank
leaf; (i) Half-title: Domnei; verso: Books by
Mr. Cabell / [followed by a list of books, the
whole enclosed in rules]; (iii) Title-page: as above;
verso: Copyright, 1913, by / Frederick A. Stokes Co. /
(*a line*) / Revised Edition, Copyright, 1920, / By
James Branch Cabell / Printed in the / United States
of America / Published, 1920 /; (v) Dedication: [as
in original edition]; verso: "The complication of opin-
ions and ideas, of / affections and habits, which prompt-
ed the cheva- / lier to devote himself to the service of a
lady, / and by which he strove to prove to her his love,
/ and to merit hers in return, was expressed, in / the
language of the Troubadours, by a single / word, by the
word *domnei*, a derivation of *domna*, / which may be
regarded as an alteration of the / Latin *domina*, lady,
mistress." / — C. C. Fauriel, / *History of Provençal
Poetry.* /; (vii-viii) Contents; (1) Divisional half-title: (*a line*) / A Preface / by / Joseph Hergesheimer /
(*a line*) /; verso: blank; 3-9, text of Preface; (10)
blank; (11) (*a line*) / Critical Comment / [followed
by seven lines of verse] / — Thomas Upcliffe. / (*a
line*) /; verso: blank; (13-14) [A note (untitled) upon Nicolas de Caen]; (15) (*a line*) / The Argument
/ [followed by the verses printed on verso of p. (v) in
the original edition] / — Sir William Allonby. / (*a

line) /; verso: (*a line*) / The Romance of Lusignan of / that forgotten maker in the / French Tongue, Messire Nicolas / de Caen. Here begins the tale / which they of Poictesme Nar- / rate concerning Dame Meli- / cent, that was daughter to / the great Count Manuel. / (*a line*) /; (17) (*a line*) / Part One / Perion / (followed by a sonnet) / (*a line*) /; verso: blank; 19-218 text.

Crown 8vo 7⅞×5: brown cloth, gilt lettering, top trimmed, otherwise uncut. Front cover: (Kalki device in lower right hand corner. Backbone: *Domnei* / (a line) / *Cabell* / *McBride* /. White end papers.

The revised text is preceded by A Preface by Joseph Hergesheimer (pp. 3-9).

(19)

FIGURES OF EARTH

Published 26 February 1921

FIGURES / OF / EARTH / A Comedy of Appearances / By / James Branch Cabell / (*a line*) / "*Cascun se mir el jove Manuel, / Qu'era del mon lo plus valens dels pros.*" / (*a line*) / New York / Robert M. McBride & Co. / 1921 /.

COLLATION: — pp. xvi×364, consisting of two blank leaves; p. (i), Half-title: Figures / of Earth /; verso: Books of Mr. Cabell / [followed by a list of books, the whole enclosed in rules]; (iii) Title-page: as above; verso: Copyright, 1921, by / James Branch Cabell / (*a line*) / Copyright 1919, 1920, by The Century Company. / Copyright, 1920, by McClure's Magazine, Inc. / Copyright, 1920, by The

Ridgway Company. / Printed in the / United States of America / (*a line*) / Published, 1921; (v) Dedication: (*a line*) / To six most gallant champions is dedicated / this history of a champion: less to repay / than to acknowledge large debts to each / of them, collectively at outset, as there- / after seriatim. / (*a line*) /; verso: blank; vii-viii, Contents; (ix) Divisional half-title: (*a line*) / A Foreword / "Amoto quæramus seria ludo." / (*a line*) / To / Sinclair Lewis. /; verso: blank; xi-xvi, text of Foreword; (1) Divisional half-title: (*a line*) / Part One / The Book of Credit / (*a line*) / To / Wilson Follett. / verso: (*a line*) / "Then answered the Sorcerer drede- / fully: Manuel, Manuel, now I shall / shewe unto thee many bokes of Nygro- / mancy, and howe thou shalt cum by it / lyghtly and knowe the practise therein. / And, moreouer, I shall shewe and in- / forme you so that thou shalt haue thy / Desyre, whereby my thynke it is a great / Gyfte for so lytyll a doynge." / (*a line*) /; 3-356 text; 357-364 blank.

Crown 8vo 7⅞×5: brown cloth, gilt lettering, top trimmed, otherwise uncut. Front cover: Kalki device, in lower right hand corner. Backbone: *Figures* / *of* / *Earth* / (a line) / *Cabell* / *McBride* /. White end papers.

Twenty-five copies of the first edition were issued altogether untrimmed, and signed by the author.

There were two other editions of this book in 1921, but these are duly described upon the copyright page as the second and third printings.

An English edition was issued in the autumn of 1921, by John Lane.

(20)
TABOO

Published March 1921

Taboo / A Legend Retold from the Dirghic of Sævius /
Nicanor, with Prolegomena, Notes, / and a Preliminary
Memoir / By / James Branch Cabell / *At melius fuerat*
non scribere, namque tacere / Tutum semper erit. / New
York / Robert M. McBride & Company / 1921 /. (*The*
title page and quotation enclosed in single red rule)

Collation: — pp. 40 (the first ten unnumbered)
consisting of p. (1), Half-title: TABOO; verso:
blank; (3) This edition is limited to nine hundred and
/ twenty numbered copies, of which one hun- / dred
copies have been signed by the author. / Copy Number
——— / (The first hundred copies were signed by the
author immediately below); verso: Books by Mr. Cabell (folllowed by a list of books, the whole enclosed
in rules); (5) Title page: as above; verso: Copyright,
1921, by / James Branch Cabell / (*a line*) / Revised
and reprinted, by permission of the / Editors, from The
Literary Review /; (7) Contents; verso: blank; (9)
Half-title: (*a line*) / The Dedication / Laudataque
virtus crescit / (*a line*) /; verso: (*a line*) / (*four lines*
of verse) / (*a line*) /; 11-13, text of dedication; (14)
Bibliographical note on The Mulberry Grove; (15)
Half-title: (*a line*) / Memoir of Sævius Nicanor /
Sævius Nicanor Marci libertus negabit / (*a line*) /;
verso: (*a line*) / (*four lines of verse*) / (*a line*); 17-
18, text of Memoir of Sævius Nicanor; (19) (*a line*)
/ Prolegomena / Nec caput habentia, nec caudam / (*a*
line) /; verso: (*a line*) / (*two lines of verse*) / (*a*
line) /; 21-40, text.

Thin demy 8vo 8⅜×5½: brown cloth, gilt lettering, top

trimmed, otherwise uncut. Front cover: (Kalki device, in lower right hand corner). Backbone lettered vertically: *Taboo — Cabell* /. White end papers.

This first edition was limited to 920 numbered copies, of which the first 100 were issued altogether untrimmed, and signed by the author.

An earlier pirated reprint of the article *The Taboo in Literature*, which comprises pp. 21-39 of the present volume, was issued in Chicago, and consists of a four-page leaflet, $9\frac{1}{2}\times7\frac{1}{2}$, unbound.

(21)

JOSEPH HERGESHEIMER

Published October 1921

JOSEPH HERGESHEIMER / An Essay in Interpretation / By / James Branch Cabell / *"And we dreamed a dream in one night, I and he: we dreamed / each man according to the interpretation of his dream."* / (*device in red*) / Chicago / The Bookfellows / 1921 /.

> COLLATION: — pp. 28 (the first 6 unnumbered), consisting of p. (1) Half-title: Joseph Hergesheimer / An Essay in Interpretation /; verso: blank; (3) Title-page: as above; verso: One thousand small paper and ninety-nine tall paper copies of this / monograph have been printed for The Bookfellows in August, 1921. / The edition is the first; Mr. Cabell the author is Bookfellow No. 513 / and Mr. Brewer the printer is Bookfellow No. 14. / Copyright 1921 by / James Branch Cabell. /; (5) To / Joseph Hergesheimer /

with friendship and large admiration / as goes the past, and with / cordial faith in what / is to come. /; verso: blank; 7-27 text; verso of p. 27, blank.

Thin 8vo 8×5¾: pamphlet, 1,000 copies, buff paper covers, black lettering, red or purple cord binding. Front cover: (design) / *Joseph* / *Hergesheimer* / *An Essay in* / *Interpretation* / (a line) / *Cabell* / (design) /

The large paper edition of ninety-nine copies is 9½×6½, bound in buff boards with black lettering. Front cover: *Joseph Hergesheimer* / (a line) / *Cabell* / This edition was the second printing, as is shown by line seventeen upon p. 25. This line in the pamphlet reads: "*one already to invest blind. Faith in what is to come very soon.*" In the large paper edition this line is corrected to: "*one already to invest blind faith in what is to come very soon.*" The copyright page states that this monograph was printed in August, 1921, but the book was not actually issued until October.

(22)

THE LINE OF LOVE

Revised version, published 15 November 1921
THE / LINE OF LOVE / Dizain des Mariages / By / James Branch Cabell / with an introduction by / H. L. Mencken / (*fleuret*) / (*four Latin lines, as in first version*) / (*fleuret*) / Robert M. McBride & Company / New York - - - - 1921 /.

COLLATION: — pp. xvi+272, consisting of (i) Half-title: The Line of Love; verso: Books by

Mr. Cabell / (followed by a list of books, the whole enclosed in rules); (iii) Title-page: as above; verso: Copyright, 1921, by / James Branch Cabell / (*a line*) / Copyright, 1905, by / Harper & Brothers / Printed in the / United States of America / (*a line*) / Published, 1921 /; (v) (*a line*) / To Robert Gamble Cabell I / (followed by six lines of verse) / (*a line*) /; verso: blank; vii-xiii, text of Introduction by H. L. Mencken; verso of p. xiii: blank; xv, Contents; verso: blank; (1) Divisional Half-title: (*a line*) / The Epistle Dedicatory / (four lines of verse) / (a line) /; verso: blank; pp. 3-261, text; (262-272) blank.

Crown 8vo 7⅞×5: brown cloth, gilt lettering, top trimmed, otherwise uncut. Front cover: (Kalki device, in lower right hand corner). Backbone: *The / Line / of / Love* / (a line) / *Cabell* / *McBride* / White end papers.

The revised text is augmented by an Introduction, by H. L. Mencken (pp. vii-xiii): The Episode Called The Wedding Jest (pp. 7-31); The Episode Called Porcelain Cups (pp. 227-253); and for the Envoi of the first version is substituted a virtually new colophon, in The Envoi Called Semper Idem (pp. 255-261).

(23)

CHIVALRY

Revised version, published 15 November 1921

CHIVALRY / Dizain des Reines / By / James Branch Cabell / with an Introduction by / Burton Rascoe /

(fleuret) / *(five line quotation, as in the first version, save that the final "and" of the fourth line is set as the beginning of the fifth)* / *(fleuret)* / Robert M. McBride & Company / New York - - - - 1921 /.

COLLATION: — pp. xvi+288, consisting of p. (i) Half-title: Chivalry /; verso: Books by Mr. Cabell / (folowed by a list of books, the whole enclosed in rules); (iii) Title-page: as above; verso: Copyright, 1921, by / James Branch Cabell / (*a line*) / Copyright, 1909, by Harper & Brothers / Printed in the / United States of America / (*a line*) / Revised and Enlarged Edition / Published October, 1921 /; (v) Dedication page (as in the original edition); verso: blank; vii-xiii, text of Introduction by Burton Rascoe; verso of p. xiii, blank; xv Contents; verso: blank; pp. 1-281, text; (282-288) blank.

Crown 8vo 7⅞×5: brown cloth, gilt, top trimmed, otherwise uncut, Front cover: (Kalki device, in lower left hand corner). Backbone: *Chivalry* / (a line) / *Cabell* / *McBride* /. White end papers.

The revised text is augmented with an Introduction by Burton Rascoe (pp. vii-xiii).

(24)

THE JEWEL MERCHANTS

Published 1 December 1921

THE JEWEL MERCHANTS / A Comedy in One Act / By / James Branch Cabell / "*Io non posso ritrar di tutti appieno:* / *pero chi si mi caccia il lungo tema,* / *che molte volte al fatto il dir vien meno.*" / New York / Robert M. McBride & Company / 1921 /. (*The title page and quotation enclosed in single red rule*)

> COLLATION:— pp. 64 (the first eight unnumbered) consisting of p. (1) Half-title: The Jewel Merchants; verso: blank; (3) This edition is limited to one thous- and and / forty numbered copies of which one hun- / dred copies have been signed by the author. / Copy Number —— / (In the first one hundred copies the author's signature immediately followed the preceding text) ; verso: Books by Mr. Cabell / (followed by a list, the whole enclosed in rules; (5) Title-page: as above; verso: Copyright, 1921, by / James Branch Cabell / (*a line*) / The acting rights to "The Jewel Merchants" are / reserved by the author, to whom application must / be made for the privilege of per- forming this play. / Printed in the / United States of America / (*a line*) / Published, 1921 /; (7) Dedica- tion page: (*a line*) / To / Louise Burleigh / This lat- est avatar of so many notions / which were originally hers. / (*a line*) /; verso: blank; 9-15: Text of The Author's Prologue; verso of p. 15: (A note upon Alessandro de Medici); (17) Half-title: (*a line*) / The Jewel Merchants / "Diamente nè smeraldo nè zaffino." / (*a line*) /; verso: List of the original cast; pp. 19-63, text; verso of 63 blank.

Thin demy 8vo 8½×5½: brown cloth, gilt lettering, whol- ly uncut.   Front cover: Kalki device, in lower right hand corner. Backbone lettered vertically: *The Jewel Mer- chants* (small triangle) *Cabell* /. White end papers.

This first edition was limited to 1,040 numbered copies, of which the first hundred copies were signed by the author.

(25)
THE LINEAGE OF LICHFIELD
Published April 1922

THE / LINEAGE OF LICHFIELD / An Essay in Eugenics / By / James Branch Cabell / . . . *atavis edite regibus, / o et præsidium et dulce decus meum* / New York / Robert M. McBride & Company / 1922 /. (*The title page and quotation enclosed in single red rule*)

COLLATION : — pp. (ii) +46 (the first eight unnumbered) consisting of, p. (i) Half-title: The Lineage of Lichfield; verso: blank; (1) This edition of The Lineage of Lichfield is / limited to three hundred and sixty-five num- / bered copies printed from type, each copy / signed by the author. / Copy Number —— / (and in the author's handwriting) *James Branch Cabell*; verso: Books by Mr. Cabell / (followed by a list, the whole enclosed in rules); (3) Title-page: as above; verso: Copyright, 1922, / by / James Branch Cabell /; (5) Half-title: The Lineage of Lichfield; verso: blank; 7-17, text of The Epistle Dedicatory; verso of p. 17: blank; (19) The Lineage of Lichfield / Being a partial list of the descendants of Dom / Manuel, Count of Poictesme, as compiled from / the books and papers of R. V. Musgrave. /; verso: genealogical note; 21-46, text.

Thin demy 8vo 8½×5½: brown cloth, gilt lettering, wholly uncut. Front cover: (Kalki device, in right hand corner). Backbone lettered vertically: *The Lineage of Lichfield — Cabell* / White end papers.

This first, and only, edition was limited to 365 copies, each numbered, and signed by the author.

(26)

GALLANTRY

Revised version, published 14 June 1922

GALLANTRY / Dizain des Fêtes Galantes / By / James Branch Cabell / with an Introduction by / Louis Untermeyer / (*a line*) / "*Half in masquerade, playing the drawing-room or / garden comedy of life, these persons have upon them, / not less than the landscape among the accidents of / which they group themselves with fittingness, a / certain light that we should seek for in vain upon / anything real.*" / (*a line*) / Robert M. McBride & Company / New York - - - - 1922 /.

COLLATION : — pp. xxii+346, consisting of p. (i) Half-title: Gallantry; verso: Books by Mr. Cabell / (followed by a list of books, the whole enclosed in rules); (iii) Title-page: as above; verso: Copyright, 1907, by / Harper & Brothers / (*a line*) / Revised Edition, / Copyright, 1922, by / James Branch Cabell / Printed in the / United States of America / (*a line*) / Published, June, 1922 /; (v) Dedication page (as in first edition); verso: blank; vii-xii, text of Introduction by Louis Untermeyer; (xiii) Contents; verso: blank; xv-xix, text of The Epistle Dedicatory; verso of p. xix: blank; xxi-xxii, text of The Prologue; (1) Half-title: (*a line*) / I / Simon's Hour / As Played at Stornoway Crag, March 25, 1750 / (six line quotation in Italics) / (*a line*) /; verso: List of Dramatis Personae; pp. 3-342, text; (343-346) blank.

Crown octavo $7\frac{7}{8} \times 5$: brown cloth, gilt lettering, top trimmed, otherwise uncut. Front cover: (Kalki device in lower right hand corner). Backbone: *Gallantry* / (a line) / *Cabell* / *McBride* /. White end papers.

The revised text has an Introduction by Louis Untermeyer (pp. vii-xii), and Contents as in first version, except that *Love's Alumni* is subheaded *The Afterpiece.*

(27)

THE CREAM OF THE JEST

Revised version, published December 1922

THE / CREAM / OF / THE JEST / (*a line*) / A Comedy of Evasions / (*a line*) / by / James Branch Cabell / with an Introduction by / Harold Ward / (*five line quotation as in first version*) / New York / Robert M. McBride & Company / 1922 /.

> COLLATION: — pp. xvi+256, consisting of p. (i) Half-title: The / Cream / of / the Jest; verso: blank; (iii) Line cut of cryptogrammatic design, as on p. (iv) of original edition; verso: List of Books by Mr. Cabell, enclosed in rectangular rule; (v) Title-page: as above; verso: Copyright, 1917, by / James Branch Cabell / (*a line*) / Printed in the / United States of America / Second Printing, January, 1920 / Third Printing, September, 1920 / Fourth Printing, September, 1921 / Fifth Printing, December, 1922 / (*a line*) / Published September, 1917 /; (vii) Dedication, as in original edition; verso: blank; ix-xii, text of Introduction by Harold Ward; xiii-xv, Contents; verso of xv: blank; (1) Half-title as in original version; verso: blank; pp. 3-250, text; (251-256) blank.

Crown octavo $7\frac{7}{8}\times5$: brown cloth, gilt lettering, top trimmed, otherwise uncut. Front cover: (Kalki device, in lower right hand corner).   Backbone: as in first version, except that the "c" in "McBride" is underlined. White end papers.

This, described on copyright page as the "Fifth Printing, December, 1922," of the novel published in 1917, is a book made from new plates, with many slight revisions and additions: and contains a preface by Harold Ward (pp. ix-xii) not included in any earlier printing.

An English edition was issued in the spring of 1923, by John Lane.   The first 1,000 copies were from imported sheets: thereafter the English publishers zinced the first version of this book, and issued it without Mr. Ward's Introduction, which the title page, bewilderingly, continued to list among the volume's contents.

(28)

THE EAGLE'S SHADOW

Revised version, published 28 August 1923

THE / EAGLE'S SHADOW / A Comedy of Purse-Strings / By / James Branch Cabell / with an introduction by / Edwin Björkman / (*a line*) / "*Ad hanc, inquam, aquilæ umbram illico pavitat / omne vulgus, contrahit sese senatus, observit / nobilitas, obsecundant judices, silent theologici, / assentantur jurisconsulti, cedunt leges, cedunt / instituta.*" / (*a line*) / Robert M. McBride & Company / New York : : : : 1923 /.

COLLATION: — pp. xl+280, consisting of p. (i), Half-title: The / Eagle's / Shadow; verso: Books by Mr.

Cabell / (followed by a list, the whole enclosed in rules; (iii) Title-page: as above; verso: Copyright, 1904, by / Doubleday, Page & Co. / Copyright, 1923, by / James Branch Cabell / (*a line*) / Printed in the / United States of America / (*a line*) / Revised Edition Published, 1923 /, (v) Dedication page: To / Martha Louise Patteson Branch / In trust that the enterprise may be judged / less by the merits of its factor / than by those of its patron. / verso: blank; vii-viii Contents: (ix) Half-title: (*a line*) / An Introduction: / Concerning Cabell / by / Edwin Björkman /; (*a line*) / verso: blank; xi-xl, text of Mr. Björkman's introduction; (1) Half-title: (*a line*) / The Eagle's Shadow / Followed by four lines of verse / (*a line*) /; verso: blank; pp. 3-250, text; (251) Half-title: (*a line*) / An Appendix: About Morals / (*followed by four lines of verse*) / (*a line*) /; verso: blank; 253-280, text of appendix.

Crown 8vo $7\frac{1}{8}\times5$: brown cloth, gilt lettering, top trimmed, otherwise uncut. Front cover: (Kalki device, in lower right hand corner. Backbone: *The / Eagle's / Shadow* / (a line) / *Cabell / McBride* / White end papers.

The revised text is augmented by An Introduction: *Concerning Cabell*, by Edwin Björkman (pp. xi-xl) and An Appendix: *About Morals* (pp. 253-280), which latter division contains a series of letters in attack and defence of the first version of this book, as these letters appeared in the *New York Times*, November, 1904 — January, 1905.

(29)

THE HIGH PLACE

Published 12 November 1923

THE HIGH PLACE: / A Comedy of Disenchantment /
by James Branch Cabell / with Illustrations and Decorations by / Frank C. Papé (*four fleurons*) / "*Build on
high place for Chemosh, the abomi-* / *nation of Moab, and
for horned Ashtoreth, the* / *abomination of Zidon, and
for Moloch, the* / *abomination of the children of Am-
mon.*" / (*drawing*) / Robert M. McBride & Company /
New York: 1923 (*three fleurons*) /.

COLLATION: — pp. x+312, (together with a frontispiece and seven pages of illustrations), consisting of p.
(i) Half-title: The / High / Place /; verso: Books by
Mr. Cabell / (followed by a list, the whole enclosed
in rules); Insert: Frontispiece, with the caption (printed on a facing tissue, in red) Florian felt himself to
be in not / quite the company suited to a noble- /
man of his rank. / See page 147 /; (iii) Title-page: as
above; verso: Copyright, 1923, by / James Branch
Cabell / Printed in the / United States of America /
This First Edition of The / High Place is limited to /
two thousand numbered copies, / of which this is /
Copy Number ——— / Published, 1923 /; (v) Dedication page: To / Robert Gamble Cabell III / this
book, where so much more is due.; verso: blank; vii-
viii, Contents; (ix) List of Illustrations; verso: blank;
(1) Half-title: (*a line*) / Part One / The End of
Long Wanting / "Lever un tel obstacle est à moy peu
de chose. / Le Ciel dèfend, de vray, certains contente-
mens; / Mais on trouve avec luy des accommodemens."
/ (*a line*) /; verso: blank; p. 3-312, text.

Demy octavo 9¾×6¼: black cloth, gilt lettering, red top, otherwise untrimmed. Front cover: *The / High Place / (design) / James Branch Cabell / Illustrated by Frank C. Papé /*. Backbone: *The / High / Place / (a line) / Cabell / McBride /*.

This edition contained pictorial end papers, a frontispiece and seven illustrations, with initial letters and tail pieces, by Frank C. Papé. This first edition was limited to 2,000 numbered copies.

With the second printing the illustrations, tail pieces and pictorial end papers were omitted, and the book was issued in the Kalki binding. Also, the quotation upon the title-page reads in this second printing, correctly, "Build an high place, &c."

In this edition the words: "With Illustrations and Decorations by Frank C. Papé" are omitted from the Title-page; upon the copyright page, the notice of the limitation of the edition is omitted, and the words, "Second Printing" are substituted; pp. (ix-x) are omitted.

An English edition, without illustrations, was issued in the November of 1923 by John Lane.

CONTRIBUTIONS TO BOOKS

JAMESTOWN TRIBUTES AND TOASTS. Edited by Julia Wyatt Bullard. Lynchburg, Va.: J. P. Bell Company, 1907. 8vo, white cloth, gilt, 196 pages. Contains: *The New Virginia*, by James Branch Cabell, p. 118. This toast was subsequently incorporated into THE RIVET IN GRANDFATHER'S NECK, and a portion of it supplies the motto upon the title page of this novel.

LITTLE VERSES AND BIG NAMES. New York: George H. Doran Company, 1915. Large 8vo, red cloth, gilt lettering. Contains: *Involuntary Sonnet to the Workers for Little Verses and Big Names* by James Branch Cabell, p. 215.

PRIZE STORIES, 1919. O. Henry Memorial Award. Garden City: Doubleday, Page & Company, 1920. 8vo, black cloth, with gilt lettering, 298 pages. Contains: *Porcelain Cups*, by James Branch Cabell, pp. 210-217. This story was subsequently incorporated into the revised version of THE LINE OF LOVE.

THE BEST SHORT STORIES OF 1919. Edited by Edward J. O'Brien. Boston: Small, Maynard & Company, 1920. 8vo, blue black cloth, gilt lettering, 414 pages. Contains: *The Wedding Jest*, by James Branch Cabell. This story was subsequently incorporated into the revised version of THE LINE OF LOVE.

JURGEN AND THE CENSOR. New York: privately printed, 1920. 8vo boards, buff cloth back and corners, paper label on backbone, 77 pages. Contains: *Preface* (pp. 7-9) and *The Judging of Jurgen* (pp. 63-64), by James Branch Cabell.

JOHAN BOJER. The Man and His Works. By Carl Gad. New York: Moffat, Yard & Company, 1920. 12mo, blue-black cloth, red lettering, 260 pages. Contains: *Critique on The Face of the World*, by James Branch Cabell, pp. 247-255.

A BIBLIOGRAPHIC CHECK LIST OF THE WORKS OF JAMES BRANCH CABELL. By Merle Johnson. New York: Frank Shay, 1921. 12mo, pamphlet, green paper covers, paper label, 28 pages. Contains: *An Epistolary Preface*, by James Branch Cabell, pp. 7-11.

THE NOVEL OF TOMORROW. By Twelve American Novelists. Indianapolis: The Bobbs-Merrill Company, 1922. Small 12mo, gray boards, brown lettering, 147 pages. Contains: *A Note on Alcoves*, by James Branch Cabell, pp. 25-35.

THE QUEEN PÉDAUQUE. By Anatole France. New York: Boni & Liveright, Inc., 1923. 16mo, flexible imitation leather, gilt lettering, 253 pages. Contains: *Introduction*, by James Branch Cabell, pp. vii-xii.

A ROUND-TABLE IN POICTESME. A Symposium. Edited by Don Bregenzer and Samuel Loveman. Privately Printed by Members of The Colophon Club, Cleveland, 1924. Demy 8vo, brown cloth, gilt lettering, 126 pages Contains: *The Author of The Eagle's Shadow*, by James Branch Cabell, pp. 5-17. Edition limited to 248 copies on vellum and 351 on Roxburghe book paper.

CONTRIBUTIONS TO PERIODICALS

THE COMEDIES OF WILLIAM CONGREVE, *The International*, April 1901. An essay, subsequently incorporated into Beyond Life.

AN AMATEUR GHOST, *The Argosy*, February, 1902. Incorporated into Jurgen.

AS PLAYED BEFORE HIS HIGHNESS, *The Smart Set*, March, 1902: included, as The Ducal Audience, in Gallantry.

LOVE-LETTERS OF FALSTAFF, *Harper's Monthly*, March, 1902: included in The Line of Love.

AFTERNOON IN ARDEN, *The Smart Set*, July, 1902: incorporated into The Cords of Vanity.

IN THE SUMMER OF ST. MARTIN, *The Smart Set*, August, 1902: included, as Love at Martinmas, in Gallantry.

"AS THE COMING OF DAWN," *The Smart Set*, September, 1902: incorporated into The Cords of Vanity.

AN INCARNATION OF HELEN, *The Smart Set*, October, 1902: incorporated into The Cords of Vanity.

THE SHADOWY PAST, *The Smart Set*, January, 1903: incorporated into The Rivet in Grandfather's Neck.

HEART OF GOLD, *The Smart Set*, February, 1903: included in Gallantry.

In Ursula's Garden, *Harper's Monthly*, May, 1903: included in The Line of Love.

The Husbands' Comedy, *The Smart Set*, June, 1903: novelette, incorporated into The Rivet in Grandfather's Neck.

The Conspiracy of Arnaye, *Harper's Monthly*, June, 1903: included in The Line of Love.

The Story of Stella, *The Smart Set*, August, 1903: incorporated into The Cords of Vanity.

The Castle of Content, *Harper's Monthly*, August, 1903: included in The Line of Love.

Old Capulet's Daughter, *The Smart Set*, September, 1903: incorporated into The Cords of Vanity.

The Awakening, *The Smart Set*, February, 1904: incorporated into The Rivet in Grandfather's Neck.

Mammon's Match, *The Smart Set*, March, 1904: incorporated into The Cords of Vanity.

The Story of Adhelmar, *Harper's Monthly*, April, 1904: included, as Adhelmar at Puysange, in The Line of Love.

The Eagle's Shadow, *The Saturday Evening Post*, nine installments, 6 August-30 September, 1904.

In Necessity's Mortar, *Harper's Monthly*, October, 1904: included in The Line of Love.

"Sweet Adelais," *Harper's Monthly*, March, 1905: included in The Line of Love.

SIMON'S HOUR, *Ainslee's Magazine*, April, 1905: included in Gallantry.

THE RHYME TO PORRINGER, *Collier's Weekly*, 15 April, 1905: included in Gallantry.

APRIL'S MESSAGE, *Ainslee's Magazine*, May, 1905: included in Gallantry.

THE FOX-BRUSH, *Harper's Monthly*, August, 1905: included in Chivalry.

THE SESTINA, *Harper's Monthly*, January, 1906: included in Chivalry.

THE CASUAL HONEYMOON, *Ainslee's Magazine*, May, 1906: included in Gallantry.

ACTORS ALL, *Appleton's Magazine*, May, 1906: included in Gallantry.

THE HOUSEWIFE, *Harper's Monthly*, August, 1906: included in Chivalry.

THE SCAPEGOATS, *Appleton's Magazine*, September, 1906: included in Gallantry.

THE TENSON, *Harper's Monthly*, December, 1906: included in Chivalry.

IN THE SECOND APRIL, *Harper's Monthly*, in two parts, April-May, 1907: included in Gallantry.

THE NAVARRESE, *Harper's Monthly*, September, 1907: included in Chivalry.

THE RAT-TRAP, *Harper's Monthly*, December, 1907: included in Chivalry.

THE CHOICES, *Harper's Monthly*, March, 1908: included in Chivalry.

THE SCABBARD, *Harper's Monthly*, May, 1908: included in Chivalry.

THE ULTIMATE MASTER, *Harper's Monthly*, November, 1908: incorporated into Domnei.

THE SATRAPS, *Harper's Monthly*, April, 1909: included in Chivalry.

A FORDYCE OF WESTBROOK, *The Red Book*, July, 1909: incorporated into The Rivet in Grandfather's Neck.

THE SECOND CHANCE, *Harper's Monthly*, October, 1909: included, as Olivia's Pottage, in The Certain Hour.

HIS RELICS, *Ainslee's Magazine*, November, 1909: incorporated into The Rivet in Grandfather's Neck.

THE SOUL OF MERVISAUNT, *Harper's Monthly*, April 1911: incorporated into Domnei.

PRINCE FRIBBLE'S BURIAL, *The Red Book*, May, 1911: included, as A Princess of Grub Street, in The Certain Hour.

CONCERNING DAVID JOGRAM, *Harper's Monthly*, November, 1911.

THE DREAM, *The Argonaut*, 23 November 1912: included, as The Lady of All Our Dreams, in The Certain Hour.

BALTHAZAR's DAUGHTER, *The Smart Set*, May, 1913: included in The Certain Hour.

VITALITY EN VOGUE, *The Sewanee Review*, January, 1915: an essay, incorporated into the Auctorial Induction of The Certain Hour.

BELHS CAVALIERS, *Lippincott's Magazine*, June, 1915: included in The Certain Hour.

JUDITH'S CREED, *Lippincott's Magazine*, July, 1915: included in The Certain Hour.

A BROWN WOMAN, *Lippincott's Magazine*, August, 1915: included in The Certain Hour.

POST ANNOS, *Poetry*, August, 1915: verses included, as One End of Love, in From the Hidden Way.

PRO HONORIA, *McBride's Magazine*, September, 1915: included in The Certain Hour.

THE IRRESISTIBLE OGLE, *McBride's*, October, 1915: included in The Certain Hour.

PASCHALIA, *Emmanuel Parish Light*, 23 April 1915: a sonnet, included, as Easter Eve, in From the Hidden Way.

A DISCOURSE FOR FRIENDS OF VIRGINIA AND CAROLINA, by Joseph Glaister, *William and Mary College Quarterly*, April, 1917: genealogical paper.

THOMAS AND WILLIAM BRANCH OF HENRICO AND SOME OF THEIR DESCENDANTS, *William and Mary College Quarterly*, October, 1917: genealogical paper.

THE TRAGEDY OF MR. TARKINGTON, *Chicago Tribune*, 6 April 1918: review of Booth Tarkington by Robert Cortes Holliday: incorporated into Beyond Life.

Branch of Henrico, *William and Mary College Quarterly*, April, 1918.

Literature and Life, *Chicago Tribune*, 14 April 1918: the first of a series of eighteen extracts from Beyond Life which appeared in this paper every Saturday, the last extract, Preferences, appearing 11 August 1918.

"Ultra Crepidam," *Chicago Tribune*, 4 May 1918.

An Epilogue, *Chicago Tribune*, 18 May 1918.

Some Ladies and Jurgen, *The Smart Set*, July, 1918: incorporated into Jurgen.

Some Morals: from the French of Villon, *The Dial*, 18 July 1918: review of The Poems of François Villon, incorporated into Beyond Life.

The Hunnicutts of Prince George, *William and Mary College Quarterly*, July and October, 1918: genealogical paper in two parts.

Rogue's March: to a Flemish Air, *The Dial*, 22 February 1919: review of The Legend of the Glorious Adventures of Tyl Ulenspiegel.

The Wedding Jest, *The Century*, September, 1919: included in the revised version of The Line of Love.

Cabell on Bojer, *New York Sun*, 12 October 1919: review of The Face of the World by Johan Bojer.

Porcelain Cups, *The Century*, November, 1919: included in the revised version of The Line of Love.

The Feathers of Olrun, *The Century*, December, 1919: incorporated into Figures of Earth.

MR. CABELL ON TURTLE-MEAT AND BROOMSTICKS, *New York Sun*, 7 December 1919: review of From a Southern Porch by Dorothy Scarborough.

IN RESPECT TO JOSEPH HERGESHEIMER, *The Bookman*, November-December (combined number), 1919: essay, incorporated into Joseph Hergesheimer.

"IT IS OF LINDA," *The Bookman*, January, 1920: review of Linda Condon, incorporated into Joseph Hergesheimer.

THE JUDGING OF JURGEN, *New York Tribune*, 8 February 1920.

THE HOUR OF FREYDIS, *McClure's Magazine*, May, 1920: incorporated into Figures of Earth.

THE HEAD OF MISERY, *McClure's Magazine*, July, 1920: incorporated into Figures of Earth.

THE DESIGNS OF MIRAMON, *The Century*, August, 1920: incorporated into Figures of Earth.

THE HAIR OF MELICENT, *McClure's Magazine*, September, 1920: incorporated into Figures of Earth.

THE IMAGE OF SESPHRA, (and letter relative to this story), *Romance*, October, 1920: incorporated into Figures of Earth.

THE TABOO IN LITERATURE, *The Literary Review*, 11 December 1920: revised and expanded into Taboo.

A POSTSCRIPT, *The Reviewer*, 15 April 1921: verse, included in Taboo.

THE DELTA OF RADEGONDE, *Vanity Fair*, June, 1921.

EXIT, *The Reviewer*, 1 June 1921: included in The Lineage of Lichfield.

THE JEWEL MERCHANTS, *The Smart Set*, July, 1921.

THE LINEAGE OF LICHFIELD, *The Reviewer*, three installments, October, November and December, 1921.

THE COMEDIAN, *Vanity Fair*, November, 1921: incorporated into the introduction to The Lineage of Lichfield.

BEAUTY AND WIZARDRY, *The Nation*, 2 November 1921: review of Messer Marco Polo by Donn Byrne.

AUTOBIOGRAPHIC SUMMARY, *The Trend*, 7 January 1922.

THE APPEAL TO POSTERITY, *The Literary Review*, 25 March 1922.

A NOTE ON ALCOVES, *The New Republic*, 12 April 1922.

THE CANDID FOOTPRINT, *The Century*, May, 1922.

THE BRIGHT BEES OF TOUPAN, *United Feature Syndicate*, published in various evening papers of 5 August, and morning papers of 6 August, 1922.

THE THIN QUEEN OF ELFHAME, *The Century*, December, 1922.

PORTRAIT OF THE ARTIST: FULL LENGTH. Review of the Carra Edition of the Collected Works of George Moore. *International Book Review*, November, 1923.

ONCE MORE, THE IMMORTALS. Review of Fantastica by Robert Nichols. *The American Mercury*, January, 1924.

ROMANTICS ABOUT THEM, *The Literary Review*, 1 March, 1924.

SOME CRITICISM IN PERIODICALS

HERE'S A CHANCE TO OWN ANOTHER FIRST EDITION. By Burton Rascoe. *Chicago Tribune*, 29 September, 1917.

AN APPROACH TO JAMES BRANCH CABELL. By Burton Rascoe. *Chicago Tribune*, 6 April 1918.

PRESUMING YOU ARE INTERESTED. By Burton Rascoe. *Chicago Tribune*, 20 April 1918.

A GOSSIP ON JAMES BRANCH CABELL. By Wilson Follett. *The Dial*, 25 April 1918.

MR. CABELL OF VIRGINIA. By H. L. Mencken. *New York Evening Mail*, 3 July 1918.

A SUB-POTOMAC PHENOMENON. By H. L. Mencken. *The Smart Set*, August, 1918.

A PERSONAL LETTER ALL MAY READ ON J. B. CABELL. By Burton Rascoe. *Chicago Tribune*, 22 May 1919.

A NEW COLOSSUS LOOMS ON THE LITERARY HORIZON. By Benjamin F. Glazer. *Philadelphia Press*, 26 October 1919.

AN IMPROVIZATION ON THEMES FROM "JURGEN." By Joseph Hergesheimer. *New York Sun*, 26 October 1919.

THE ROMANTIC IRONY OF CABELL. By Benjamin de Casseres. *New York Evening Post*, 26 June 1920.

THE ART OF JAMES BRANCH CABELL. By Hugh Walpole. *The Yale Review*, July, 1920.

DISCOVERED BY THE CENSOR. By Gregory Stagnell. *New York Medical Journal*, 24 July 1920.

JAMES BRANCH CABELL: AN INTRODUCTION. By John J. Gunther. *The Bookman*, November, 1920.

MR. CABELL OF VIRGINIA. Anonymous. *The Double-Dealer*. January, 1921.

JAMES BRANCH CABELL: PROSPERO. By Benjamin de Casseres. *Shadowland*, February, 1921.

JAMES BRANCH CABELL, "Master of the Pastiche." By Richard le Gallienne. *New York Times*, 13 February 1921.

JAMES BRANCH CABELL, Master of Shady Romance. Anonymous. *Kansas City Star*, 19 February, 1921.

A NOTE ON JAMES BRANCH CABELL. By J. A. Thomas. *Yale Literary Magazine*, March, 1921.

MR. JAMES BRANCH CABELL. By Robert Morss Lovett. *The New Republic*, 13 April 1921.

THE ESSENTIALS OF NONSENSE. By Maurice Hewlett. *The Literary Review*, 23 April 1921.

JAMES BRANCH CABELL. (By Frances Newman.) *Carnegie Library Quarterly*, May, 1921.

ONE ON A TOWER. By H. B. Fuller. *The Freeman*, May, 1921.

IMPRESSIONS OF AMERICAN LITERATURE: III. James Branch Cabell. By C. E. Bechoffer. *London Times*, 16 June 1921.

CONTEMPORARY AMERICAN NOVELISTS: VI. James Branch Cabell. By Carl Van Doren. *The Nation*, 29 June 1921.

CRITICIZING THE CRITIC. By John S. Sumner. *The Bookman*, July, 1921.

JAMES BRANCH CABELL: AUTHOR OF "JURGEN." By Roy L. McCardell. *New York Morning Telegraph*, 21 August 1921.

THE PASSING OF JAMES BRANCH CABELL. By Vincent Starrett. *The Double-Dealer*, November, 1921.

THE MODERNISM OF MR. CABELL. By John Peale Bishop. *Vanity Fair*, March, 1922.

JAMES BRANCH CABELL. By Maud Skidmore Barber. *The Book Scorpion*, March, 1922.

CABELL IN 1904. By Thomas Caldecot Chubb. *New York Tribune*, 7 May 1922.

A KEY TO CABELL. By Louis Untermeyer. *The Double-Dealer*, June, 1922.

A NOTE ON JAMES BRANCH CABELL. By Burton Rascoe. *New York Tribune*, 6 August 1922.

CONCERNING JAMES BRANCH CABELL'S HUMAN COMEDY. By Edwin Björkman. *International Book Review*, December, 1922.

JURGEN IN LIMBO. By Carl Van Doren. *The Nation*, 6 December 1922.

THE LITERARY SPOTLIGHT: XVI. James Branch Cabell. (By Edward Hale Bierstadt.) *The Bookman*, February, 1923.

A NEW GENIUS OF LETTERS. By S. P. B. Mais. *Sunday Express*, London, 6 May 1923.

JAMES BRANCH CABELL: Romancer and Apostle of Disillusion. By N. T. *Aberdeen* (Scotland) *Press and Journal*, 14 May 1923.

JAMES BRANCH CABELL. By Irene Byrne Chamberlin. *The Chicago Woman's Club Bulletin*, May 1923.

"JURGEN" AND THE JUDGES. By Joseph Shearing. *Cassell's Weekly*, London, 27 June 1923.

LES DERNIÈRES PUBLICATIONS AMÉRICAINES: James Branch Cabell. *L'Europe Nouvelle*, Paris, 30 June, 1923.

ANOTHER NOTE ON CABELL. By Aleister Crowley. *The Reviewer*, July 1923.

MR. CABELL. *The Triad*, Sydney, Australia, 10 August 1923.

NIEUWE ENGELSCHE BOEKEN: James Branch Cabell. By Augusta De Wit. *Nieuwen Rotterdamsche Courant.* Holland, 15 September 1923.

"THE CREAM OF THE JEST." Anonymous. *Allahabad* (India) *Pioneer*, 23 September 1923.

AN AFFIRMATION. By Richard Montgomery. *The New Age*, London, 27 November 1923.

CABELL IN GEORGIA: The Aristocrat of Letters. By H. W. S. *Cassell's Weekly*, London, 15 December 1923.

JAMES BRANCH CABELL. By Stanley E. Babb. *Galveston* (Texas) *News*, 16 December 1923.

THE BEAUTIFUL HAPPENING. By Hunter Stagg. *The Reviewer*, January 1924.

JURGEN THE POET. Anonymous. *The New Age*, London, 10 January 1924.

SOME CRITICISM IN BOOKS

The Men Who Make Our Novels. By George Gordon. Contains: *Chapter XVIII — James Branch Cabell*, pp. 113-118. New York, Moffat, Yard & Company, 1919.

The Art of James Branch Cabell. By Hugh Walpole. With an Appendix of Individual Comment upon the Cabell Books. New York, Robert M. McBride & Company, 1920.

Our Short Story Writers. By Blanche Colton Williams, Ph.D. Contains: *Chapter II — James Branch Cabell*, pp. 22-40. New York, Moffat, Yard & Company, 1920.

Letters on Contemporary American Authors. By Martin MacCollough. Contains: *Letter I.* (on James Branch Cabell), pp. 7-12. Boston, The Four Seas Company, 1921.

Modern American Poetry. By Louis Untermeyer. Contains: *James Branch Cabell*, pp. 213-214. New York: Harcourt, Brace & Co., 1921.

Contemporary American Novelists, 1900-1920. By Carl Van Doren. Contains: *James Branch Cabell*, pp. 104-112. New York, The Macmillan Company, 1922.

Das Grosse Bestiarium der Modernen Literatur. By Franz Blei. Contains: *Cabell*, p. 25. Berlin, Ernst Rowohlt Verlag, 1922.

Jurgen and the Law. A Statement, With Exhibits, Including the Court's Opinion and the Brief for the Detendants on Motion to Direct an Acquittal. Edited by Guy Holt. New York, Robert M. McBride & Company, 1923.

The Literary Renaissance in America. By C. E. Bechoffer. Pp. 42-56 devoted to James Branch Cabell. London, Wm. Heinemann Ltd., 1923.

Buried Cæsars. By Vincent Starrett. Contains: *The Passing of James Branch Cabell*, pp. 87-104. Chicago: Covici-McGee Co., 1923.

On Strange Altars. By Paul Jordan-Smith. Contains: *James Branch Cabell*, pp. 200-213. New York: Albert & Charles Boni, 1924.

A Round-Table in Poictesme. A Symposium, Edited by Don Bregenzer and Samuel Loveman. Contains thirteen papers upon various aspects of Mr. Cabell's work, by James Branch Cabell, Ernest Boyd, Don Bregenzer, Samuel Loveman, Frank L. Minarik, Ben Ray Redman, M. P. Mooney, Christopher Morley, Edwin Meade Robinson, Howard Wolf, H. L. Mencken, Burton Rascoe, and Carr Liggett. The Colophon Club, Cleveland, O., 1924.

*   *   *   *   *   *

A Parody Outline of History. By Donald Ogden Stewart. Contains: *Cristofer Colombo: A Comedy of Discovery: In the Manner of James Branch Cabell*, pp. 25-54. New York, George H. Doran Company, 1921.

Heavens. By Louis Untermeyer. Contains: *The Heaven above Storysende*, pp. 49-60. New York, Harcourt, Brace & Company, 1922.

FUTURE COLLATIONS

FUTURE COLLATIONS

FUTURE COLLATIONS

FUTURE COLLATIONS

FUTURE COLLATIONS

FUTURE COLLATIONS